Author biography

Hi I am Arindam. Having worked for corporate training for more than a decade, I realize that writing a book about ADDIE is going to help a lot of people who are seeking a carrer in the training industry and wants to learn more about the content creation.

This is my first book about Instructoional Designing and ADDIE and I would like to apologize to everyone if the expectation is not met about this book. I have worked with multiple organizations and have helped them with their online course designing.

I have also helped more than 3000 trainers to shape their carrer towards a better learning and understanding of the Instructional Designing.

If you would like to keep in touch with me, please feel free to drop an email at trainercentric@gmail.com and I will get back to you as soon as I can.

Cheerio...

Until next time,

Arindam

CONTENTS

Introduction to Instructional Design 11

Analyzing the Learning Needs 14

Designing Effective Learning Objectives 17

Developing Engaging Instructional Materials 20

Implementing Instructional Strategies 23

Evaluating and Assessing Learning Outcomes 26

Iterating and Enhancing Instruction 29

Reflecting and Iterating in Instructional Design 31

Gamification in Instructional Design 34

Gamification Strategies for Effective Learning 37

The Power of Instructional Design 43

Implementing Effective Instructional Strategies 46

Leveraging Technology for Enhanced
Learning Experiences 49

Cultivating Inclusive Learning Environments 52

Assessing Learning Outcomes 55

Evaluating Instructional Design Effectiveness 58

Collaborative Learning and Instructional Design 61

Measuring the Impact of Instructional Design 65

Continuous Improvement in Instructional Design 69

Final Thoughts 73

Designing Impactful Learning

Arindam Mondal

ISBN 978-93-5667-880-4
© Arindam Mondal 2023

Published in India 2023 by Pencil

A brand of

One Point Six Technologies Pvt. Ltd.
Unit no. 26, Ground Floor, Building A1,
Wadala Truck Terminal Road,
Near Post Office, Antop Hill, Mumbai - 400037
E connect@thepencilapp.com
W www.thepencilapp.com

All rights reserved worldwide

No part of this publication may be reproduced, stored in or introduced into a retrieval system, or transmitted, in any form, or by any means (electronic, mechanical, photocopying, recording, or otherwise), without the prior written permission of the Publisher. Any person who commits an unauthorized act in relation to this publication can be liable to criminal prosecution and civil claims for damages.

DISCLAIMER: *The opinions expressed in this book are those of the authors and do not purport to reflect the views of the Publisher.*

Facilitating Collaborative Learning 75

Epigraph

As we reach the final pages of this book on the ADDIE method of instructional design, we find ourselves at the crossroads of reflection and anticipation. It has been a journey filled with emotional depth, a journey that has invited us to embrace the artistry and impact of instructional design. Now, as we turn our gaze towards the horizon of possibilities, let us take a moment to reflect on the profound impact of this journey and the lasting imprint it leaves on our hearts and minds.

Throughout this book, we have explored the stages of the ADDIE method, from analysis and design to development, implementation, evaluation, and iteration. We have delved into the emotional dimensions of each stage, recognizing that behind every instructional design lies a human connection—an opportunity to inspire, empower, and transform lives. We have discovered that instructional design is not merely a process; it is a calling— a calling to serve, to ignite curiosity, and to shape the future of education.

In the chapters that unfolded before us, we embraced the emotional tapestry of instructional design. We learned to listen deeply to the needs and aspirations of our learners, to create inclusive and engaging learning experiences, and to cultivate a culture of empathy, resilience, and growth. We navigated the intricate dance of instructional delivery, fostering connections and inspiring a love for learning. We celebrated the power of assessment, recognizing its role in nurturing confidence, growth mindset, and self-reflection. We embarked on a journey of iteration and enhancement, embracing change, and pursuing excellence. And finally, we acknowledged the transformative power of instructional design, its ability to shape minds, hearts, and the world.

But as we bid farewell to these pages, let us remember that the journey does not end here. It is but a beginning—a beginning of a lifelong commitment to learning, growth, and impact. Instructional design is not confined to the boundaries of a book; it lives and breathes within the classrooms, the communities, and the hearts of educators and learners alike. It is a journey of heart and purpose, one that extends beyond the pages and into the very fabric of our lives.

So, dear reader, as you close this book, may you carry with you the lessons learned, the insights gained, and the passion kindled within your heart. May you continue to explore, to innovate, and to advocate for a transformative education that nurtures the potential and empowers learners to create a better world. Let the principles of the ADDIE method guide your path, reminding you of the profound impact you have as an instructional designer.

Remember, the work you do is more than a profession—it is a calling, a vocation of the heart. Embrace it with love, compassion, and a deep belief in the power of education to shape lives and ignite change. Your journey as an instructional designer has only just begun, and the world eagerly awaits the imprint you will leave on the hearts and minds of those you touch.

Thank you for embarking on this emotional odyssey with us. May your journey be filled with purpose, fulfillment, and a profound sense of joy as you continue to shape the future of education through the power of instructional design.

With heartfelt gratitude,

Arindam

Preface

Welcome to "Mastering Instructional Design: A Journey through the ADDIE Method." In this book, we will embark on an inspiring exploration of the ADDIE method, a proven framework for creating effective and impactful learning experiences. As we delve into the intricacies of instructional design, we will discover how this systematic approach can empower educators and instructional designers to craft engaging and transformative learning journeys.

The ADDIE method, which stands for Analysis, Design, Development, Implementation, and Evaluation, provides a solid foundation for designing instruction that meets the diverse needs of learners. Throughout this book, we will unravel each stage of the ADDIE process, unraveling its essence and equipping you with the knowledge and skills necessary to become a proficient instructional designer.

But this book is more than just a technical guide. It is a passionate exploration of the art and science behind effective instructional design. We will delve into the emotional aspects of learning and discover how to create experiences that ignite curiosity, inspire engagement, and foster a love for lifelong learning. By infusing our instructional design with empathy, creativity, and a deep understanding of human psychology, we can truly transform education and empower learners to reach their full potential.

Each chapter will take you on a captivating journey, combining theoretical insights with practical examples and real-life case studies. You will gain a comprehensive understanding of the ADDIE method and its application in diverse educational settings. Moreover, you will learn how to leverage emerging technologies, embrace learner-centered approaches, and cultivate an inclusive and collaborative learning environment.

As you immerse yourself in the chapters ahead, prepare to be moved, motivated, and inspired. Instructional design is not merely a technical process; it is a transformative endeavor that has the power to shape lives and create a better future. Let this book be your guide as we embark on an emotional and enlightening expedition into the realm of instructional design, where passion meets purpose, and learning becomes a deeply meaningful experience.

Introduction to Instructional Design

Chapter 1: Introduction to Instructional Design

Amidst the vast landscape of education, where knowledge intertwines with dreams and aspirations, lies a realm of boundless possibilities—welcome to the world of instructional design. In this chapter, we embark on an emotional journey that unearths the very essence of this transformative field. It is a journey that will ignite a spark within you, fueling your passion for shaping minds and inspiring hearts.

As we step into the realm of instructional design, let us pause for a moment to reflect on the power that education holds. Education has the ability to elevate individuals, to breathe life into their dreams, and to illuminate the path toward a brighter future. It is a beacon of hope, a gateway to opportunity, and a catalyst for change. Instructional design, at its core, is the art of crafting the educational experiences that have the potential to change lives.

Imagine a world where learning transcends the confines of traditional classrooms and textbooks—a world where education becomes a symphony of emotions, where students are not mere recipients of information, but active participants in their own journey of discovery. Instructional design is the key that unlocks this world, allowing us to create immersive and engaging learning experiences that resonate deep within the hearts and minds of learners.

As instructional designers, we become architects of knowledge, carefully designing each element of the learning experience to evoke emotion, curiosity, and wonder. We understand that learning is not a cold, sterile process but a deeply human one. It is an emotional endeavor that requires empathy, understanding, and a genuine connection with learners.

In this chapter, we will delve into the foundations of instructional design. We will explore the principles that guide our craft and the methodologies that shape our approach. We will unravel the importance of understanding learner needs, motivations, and aspirations—the very fabric that forms the tapestry of effective instructional design.

But beyond the technicalities, we will also delve into the emotional core of instructional design. We will explore the joy that comes from witnessing a student's "aha" moment, the pride that swells within us when we witness growth and progress, and the profound sense of fulfillment that comes from knowing that we have made a difference in someone's life.

Instructional design is a calling—an opportunity to ignite the flame of curiosity, to nurture the thirst for knowledge, and to empower learners to become architects of their own destinies. It is a responsibility that requires not only expertise but also heart and soul. Through this book, we will embark on a shared journey—a journey that embraces the emotional dimensions of instructional design and invites you to bring your unique voice and passion to the process.

So, let us take the first step on this emotional odyssey—a journey that will awaken your spirit, inspire your creativity, and immerse you in the profound impact that instructional design can have on the lives of learners. Together, we will discover the power of education to touch hearts, transform minds, and create a future where every individual can thrive and shine.

In the next chapter, we will venture into the first stage of the ADDIE method—Analyzing the Learning Needs. Get ready to explore the intricacies of understanding learners on a deep and emotional level, as we lay the foundation for designing meaningful and impactful learning experiences.

Analyzing the Learning Needs

Chapter 2: Analyzing the Learning Needs

Within the depths of every learner lies a unique story—a tapestry of experiences, hopes, and dreams that shape their individual learning needs. In this chapter, we embark on an emotional exploration of the crucial stage of instructional design—Analyzing the Learning Needs. It is a journey that invites us to empathize, to listen deeply, and to unravel the intricate threads of each learner's story.

As instructional designers, we understand that learning is not a one-size-fits-all endeavor. Each learner comes to us with their own set of challenges, aspirations, and background knowledge. To truly design instruction that resonates and connects, we must first embrace the power of empathy. We must open our hearts and minds to the realities faced by our learners, and in doing so, we can uncover the true essence of their learning needs.

Imagine a young student who struggles with self-confidence, grappling with the fear of failure that looms heavy upon their shoulders. Or an adult learner, juggling the responsibilities of work and family, yearning for a flexible learning experience that fits into the chaotic rhythm of their life. Every learner carries within them a unique set of emotional challenges and personal circumstances that shape their readiness to learn.

In the process of analyzing learning needs, we become detectives, uncovering the clues that reveal the intricate tapestry of each learner's story. We engage in meaningful conversations, conduct interviews, and seek to understand the emotional landscape that influences their learning journey. Through this process, we gain insights into their motivations, strengths, and areas of growth, allowing us to tailor our instruction to meet their specific needs.

But analyzing learning needs goes beyond gathering data and statistics. It requires us to step into the shoes of our learners, to feel the weight of their challenges, and to celebrate their triumphs. We must become not only observers but also active listeners, creating a safe space for learners to share their aspirations, doubts, and fears. It is through these moments of vulnerability and connection that we can truly understand the emotional nuances that underpin their learning needs.

As we collect and analyze the puzzle pieces of our learners' stories, we must also remember that we are not alone in this journey. Collaboration becomes an integral part of understanding and meeting learning needs. We engage with fellow educators, administrators, and even the learners themselves, fostering a collective effort to create an inclusive and supportive learning environment.

In this chapter, we will explore the methodologies and tools that enable us to analyze learning needs with emotional depth and insight. We will delve into techniques such as learner interviews, surveys, and observations, seeking to uncover the emotional landscapes that shape the learning process. Through real-life case studies and practical examples, we will witness the transformative power of analyzing learning needs to create instruction that touches hearts and sparks meaningful growth.

So, let us embrace the profound responsibility that comes with analyzing learning needs. Let us embark on a journey of empathy, curiosity, and connection—an emotional expedition that will enable us to design instruction that not only imparts knowledge but also nurtures the souls of our learners. Together, we will weave a tapestry of learning experiences that celebrate the uniqueness of each learner, empower their dreams, and create a world where education becomes a beacon of hope and possibility.

In the next chapter, we will dive into the second stage of the ADDIE method—Designing Effective Learning Objectives. Get ready to harness the emotional energy of learning needs analysis and channel it into crafting transformative objectives that guide our instructional design journey.

Designing Effective Learning Objectives

In the vast realm of education, learning objectives serve as guiding stars, illuminating the path toward meaningful growth and transformation. In this chapter, we embark on an emotional exploration of the art of designing effective learning objectives. It is a journey that embraces the power of clarity, intention, and vision—an opportunity to ignite the flames of inspiration within both educators and learners alike.

As instructional designers, we understand that learning objectives are more than just statements of what students will learn. They are beacons of purpose, encapsulating the hopes and aspirations we hold for our learners. Each objective carries within it a promise—an invitation to embark on a journey of discovery, empowerment, and personal growth.

Close your eyes for a moment and envision the transformative power of a well-crafted learning objective. Imagine a young mind, previously disengaged and disheartened, suddenly ignited with curiosity and excitement as they grasp the clear direction and purpose of their learning journey. Picture an adult learner, burdened by self-doubt, finding renewed confidence and motivation as they connect their aspirations to tangible, actionable objectives.

Designing effective learning objectives is an emotional endeavor—a delicate dance between articulating high expectations and instilling a sense of possibility. It requires us to tap into the passions and dreams of our learners, aligning our objectives with their innate desires for growth and achievement. By doing so, we infuse the learning experience with emotional resonance, fostering a deep sense of ownership and commitment.

In this chapter, we will explore the art of crafting learning objectives that inspire and empower. We will delve into the process of distilling complex educational goals into clear and concise statements, making the path ahead visible and attainable. Through the power of language, we will evoke emotions and kindle motivation, setting the stage for transformative learning experiences.

But designing effective learning objectives is not a solitary pursuit. It is a collaborative endeavor that involves engaging learners, fellow educators, and stakeholders in the process. By incorporating diverse perspectives and embracing collective wisdom, we enrich the emotional fabric of our objectives, ensuring they resonate deeply with the needs and aspirations of our learners.

Moreover, the process of designing learning objectives is not static; it is an iterative and reflective journey. As we progress through the ADDIE method, we continuously revisit and refine our objectives, adjusting our course to meet the evolving needs and emotional landscapes of our learners. This adaptability allows us to foster a dynamic and responsive learning environment, where objectives remain grounded in empathy and connection.

So, let us embark on this emotional quest of designing effective learning objectives. Let us embrace the power of intention, clarity, and inspiration as we craft the compass that will guide our learners toward their full potential. Together, we will create a tapestry of objectives that stirs emotions, ignites passions, and transforms learning into a deeply meaningful and enriching experience.

In the next chapter, we will venture into the fourth stage of the ADDIE method—Developing Engaging Instructional Materials. Get ready to breathe life into learning, as we explore the creative and emotional dimensions of instructional design.

Developing Engaging Instructional Materials

In the realm of instructional design, the materials we create are not merely vessels of information. They are the very essence of our passion and creativity—an opportunity to weave a tapestry of engagement, inspiration, and emotional connection. In this chapter, we embark on an emotional journey as we explore the art of developing engaging instructional materials. It is a journey that invites us to unleash our imaginations, to embrace our inner artists, and to craft experiences that resonate deeply with learners.

Imagine a classroom where the walls come alive with vibrant colors, where the touch of a book transports students to new worlds, and where technology seamlessly integrates with the magic of human connection. Visualize the joy in a child's eyes as they hold a beautifully illustrated storybook, the anticipation that fills a learner's heart as they embark on an interactive digital module, or the profound impact of a well-crafted video that brings concepts to life. Instructional materials have the power to awaken emotions, evoke wonder, and ignite the sparks of curiosity within each learner.

Developing engaging instructional materials is an emotional act of creation. It requires us to channel our deepest passions, to infuse our materials with our own enthusiasm and love for learning. As instructional designers, we become artists, shaping experiences that transcend the boundaries of traditional education. We blend the visual, auditory, and tactile elements into a symphony of emotions, captivating learners' hearts and minds.

In this chapter, we will explore the creative process of developing instructional materials that inspire, engage, and connect. We will unlock the secrets of storytelling, harnessing its power to transport learners to new dimensions of understanding. We will harness the potential of multimedia, leveraging images, videos, and audio to create immersive and memorable learning experiences.

But beyond the technical aspects, we will also delve into the emotional core of developing instructional materials. We will uncover the secrets of empathy, designing materials that honor the diverse needs, interests, and backgrounds of our learners. We will cultivate an environment where creativity thrives, where we tap into the wellspring of our own emotions to craft materials that resonate deeply with our audience.

Moreover, the development of instructional materials is an opportunity for collaboration and community-building. We engage with learners, fellow educators, and experts in the field, seeking their insights and feedback to shape our materials into powerful conduits of emotional connection and knowledge transfer. Through collective wisdom and shared experiences, we elevate our materials to new heights, infusing them with the richness of diverse perspectives.

So, let us embark on this emotional voyage of developing engaging instructional materials. Let us unleash our imaginations, ignite our creativity, and honor the transformative power of design. Together, we will create a tapestry of materials that go beyond the ordinary, sparking joy, curiosity, and a love for lifelong learning.

In the next chapter, we will dive into the fifth stage of the ADDIE method—Implementing Instructional Strategies. Get ready to bring our materials to life, as we explore the emotional dimensions of instructional delivery and create transformative learning experiences.

Implementing Instructional Strategies

In the heart of every classroom, a symphony of voices, dreams, and possibilities awaits. It is here, in the act of implementing instructional strategies, that we breathe life into our carefully crafted materials and create a sacred space for transformative learning experiences. In this chapter, we embark on an emotional journey, embracing the role of facilitators, mentors, and guides as we explore the art of instructional delivery.

Close your eyes for a moment and imagine the energy that fills the room as learners gather, their hearts brimming with anticipation and curiosity. Envision the profound responsibility that rests upon your shoulders as you step into the role of an instructional leader—the guardian of knowledge, the weaver of dreams, and the catalyst for growth. It is within your hands that the power to inspire, ignite, and empower resides.

Implementing instructional strategies is an emotional act of connection—a dance between educator and learner, where trust, empathy, and engagement intertwine. It is a delicate balance of structure and flexibility, where we create a safe and inclusive environment that nurtures the emotional well-being and intellectual curiosity of our learners.

As instructional designers, we understand that effective instructional delivery goes beyond the transmission of information. It requires us to foster deep connections with our learners, to see them not as passive recipients but as active participants in their own learning journey. We honor their individuality, their strengths, and their unique perspectives, and we invite them to co-create knowledge with us.

In this chapter, we will explore the emotional dimensions of instructional delivery. We will dive into the art of active listening, cultivating an environment where every voice is heard and valued. We will tap into the power of empathy, responding to the emotional needs of our learners and creating a sense of belonging and trust. Through effective questioning and facilitation techniques, we will ignite critical thinking, curiosity, and self-reflection.

But beyond the strategies, we will also delve into the emotional landscape of the learning environment. We will create a classroom culture that celebrates growth, resilience, and a love for learning. We will nurture the emotional well-being of our learners, recognizing that their socio-emotional development is intricately linked to their academic success. By fostering a culture of kindness, empathy, and collaboration, we create a fertile ground where deep learning can take root.

Moreover, implementing instructional strategies is a journey of continuous growth and reflection. We adapt and refine our approaches based on the emotional feedback received from our learners, always seeking to meet their evolving needs and aspirations. We embrace the vulnerability of self-reflection, inviting feedback from our learners and colleagues, and acknowledging that our own emotional well-being and growth are intertwined with the success of our instructional delivery.

So, let us embark on this emotional voyage of implementing instructional strategies. Let us step into the role of a guide, an advocate, and a mentor, as we create transformative learning experiences that empower our learners to reach for the stars. Together, we will build a community of learners who believe in their own potential, who embrace the joy of discovery, and who carry the torch of knowledge into the world.

In the next chapter, we will delve into the sixth stage of the ADDIE method—Evaluating and Assessing Learning Outcomes. Get ready to embark on a journey of reflection, growth, and celebration, as we explore the emotional dimensions of measuring learning success.

Evaluating and Assessing Learning Outcomes

In the tapestry of education, evaluation and assessment serve as the threads that weave together the story of growth, progress, and achievement. In this chapter, we embark on a journey of reflection, celebration, and emotional discovery as we explore the art of evaluating and assessing learning outcomes. It is a chapter that invites us to honor the journey of our learners, to acknowledge their accomplishments, and to embrace the transformative power of feedback.

As instructional designers, we understand that assessment is more than just a measure of knowledge. It is an opportunity to nurture a growth mindset, to instill confidence, and to empower learners to take ownership of their learning journey. Each assessment moment is an emotional crossroad—a chance for learners to showcase their progress, to reflect on their strengths, and to identify areas for growth.

Close your eyes and imagine the pride and joy that radiate from a learner's face as they receive positive feedback on a project they poured their heart and soul into. Envision the resilience and determination that arise within a student as they receive constructive feedback, seeing it as an opportunity to improve and grow. Assessment moments have the power to shape learners' self-perception, their motivation, and their belief in their own potential.

In this chapter, we will delve into the emotional dimensions of evaluating and assessing learning outcomes. We will explore the art of providing feedback that inspires, motivates, and fosters a sense of belonging. We will embrace the power of formative assessment, creating a continuous feedback loop that guides learners' progress and celebrates their achievements.

But beyond the techniques, we will also journey into the emotional landscape of evaluation and assessment. We will create an environment where mistakes are seen as stepping stones to success, where learners feel safe to take risks and embrace challenges. We will cultivate a culture of growth, where learners are encouraged to reflect on their own progress, set goals, and take ownership of their learning.

Moreover, the evaluation and assessment process is not a solitary act. It is a collaborative endeavor that involves learners, educators, and even the broader community. We engage in dialogues, conferences, and portfolio reviews, creating opportunities for learners to articulate their growth, share their successes, and receive guidance and support. Through this collective effort, we foster a sense of connection and collective responsibility for learning outcomes.

So, let us embark on this emotional journey of evaluating and assessing learning outcomes. Let us celebrate the growth, the perseverance, and the transformation of our learners. Together, we will create an assessment process that goes beyond numbers and scores, nurturing the emotional well-being and inspiring a lifelong love for learning.

In the next chapter, we will venture into the final stage of the ADDIE method—Iterating and Enhancing Instruction. Get ready to embark on a path of continuous improvement and emotional connection as we explore the power of reflection, adaptation, and innovation in instructional design.

Iterating and Enhancing Instruction

In the realm of instructional design, the journey never truly ends. It is a perpetual cycle of reflection, adaptation, and innovation—an eternal dance of growth and improvement. In this chapter, we embrace the power of iteration and enhancement as we explore the emotional dimensions of refining our instructional design. It is a chapter that beckons us to embrace change, to listen to the whispers of our learners, and to strive for excellence.

As instructional designers, we understand that the needs of our learners evolve, the educational landscape shifts, and new possibilities emerge. It is within this space of continuous improvement that we find the opportunity to breathe new life into our instructional designs, infusing them with relevance, engagement, and emotional resonance.

Imagine a world where every classroom is a living laboratory—a space where ideas are born, tested, and refined. Envision the excitement and anticipation that fill the air as educators collaborate, experiment, and push the boundaries of traditional teaching. It is within this dynamic environment that we discover the transformative power of iteration—an emotional journey of growth and discovery.

In this chapter, we will delve into the art of iterating and enhancing instruction. We will explore the power of reflection, carving out moments of introspection to assess the effectiveness of our designs. We will embrace the insights and feedback from learners, fellow educators, and stakeholders, infusing our designs with their perspectives and aspirations.

But beyond the process, we will also venture into the emotional landscape of iteration. We will let go of attachment to the familiar, embracing the discomfort of change and uncertainty. We will celebrate the courage to take risks, to challenge conventions, and to venture into uncharted territories. Through this emotional resilience, we uncover the hidden gems of innovation and inspiration, breathing new life into our instructional designs.

Moreover, the journey of iteration and enhancement is not a solitary path. It is a collaborative endeavor that calls upon the collective wisdom and shared experiences of our learning communities. We engage in professional learning networks, seek mentorship, and participate in communities of practice, nurturing a culture of support, innovation, and continuous growth.

So, let us embark on this emotional voyage of iterating and enhancing instruction. Let us embrace the ebb and flow of change, as we strive to create designs that captivate hearts, inspire minds, and transform lives. Together, we will shape the future of education, infusing it with a passion for lifelong learning and a commitment to excellence.

In the next chapter, we will conclude our journey through the ADDIE method. Get ready to embrace the fullness of this emotional odyssey as we reflect on the power of instructional design in shaping the world of education.

Reflecting and Iterating in Instructional Design

In this final chapter, we delve into the importance of reflection and iteration in the instructional design process. We recognize that continuous improvement is essential for creating effective and impactful learning experiences, and reflection serves as a catalyst for growth and innovation.

Reflection allows instructional designers to critically examine their design choices, strategies, and outcomes. It involves thoughtful analysis, self-assessment, and consideration of feedback from learners, colleagues, and stakeholders. By taking the time to reflect on the strengths and weaknesses of their instructional design, instructional designers gain valuable insights that inform future iterations and improvements.

One of the key benefits of reflection is the opportunity for professional growth and development. Through reflection, instructional designers deepen their understanding of instructional theories, research-based practices, and emerging trends in education. They gain a deeper awareness of their own instructional design process, strengths, and areas for improvement. This self-reflection promotes a growth mindset, a commitment to lifelong learning, and a dedication to staying abreast of current best practices in the field.

Reflection also allows instructional designers to gain a learner's perspective. By putting themselves in the shoes of the learners, they can better empathize with their needs, motivations, and challenges. This learner-centered approach informs instructional design decisions, ensuring that the design is relevant, engaging, and meaningful to the intended audience. Through reflection, instructional designers can identify areas where adjustments are needed to better align the instructional design with the learners' expectations and requirements.

Another important aspect of reflection is the identification and celebration of successes and achievements. By acknowledging the positive impact of their instructional design, instructional designers reinforce their sense of purpose and motivation. Recognizing the positive outcomes and the transformative experiences their design has facilitated boosts confidence, encourages further innovation, and inspires instructional designers to continue their pursuit of excellence.

Iteration is the natural outcome of reflection in the instructional design process. It involves making thoughtful revisions, refinements, and enhancements based on the insights gained through reflection. Instructional designers iterate by incorporating feedback, adjusting instructional strategies, and refining learning materials. This iterative approach ensures that the instructional design remains dynamic, responsive, and aligned with the evolving needs of learners and the changing educational landscape.

Technology plays a significant role in facilitating reflection and iteration. Digital tools and platforms offer instructional designers opportunities for collaboration, sharing ideas, and gathering feedback from a diverse range of stakeholders. Online communities, social media, and professional networks provide spaces for instructional designers to connect, share experiences, and learn from each other. Technology also enables instructional designers to gather data, analyze learner interactions, and identify areas for improvement, facilitating evidence-based decision-making during the iteration process.

In conclusion, reflection and iteration are vital components of the instructional design process. Through reflection, instructional designers gain valuable insights into their design choices, learner needs, and their own professional growth. By embracing an iterative approach, instructional designers continuously refine and improve their instructional designs to create meaningful, engaging, and effective learning experiences. Reflection and iteration foster innovation, promote learner-centered design, and ensure that instructional designers remain at the forefront of educational practices. By valuing reflection and iteration, instructional designers have the power to shape the future of education and positively impact the lives of learners.

Gamification in Instructional Design

In this chapter, we explore the concept of gamification in instructional design and its potential to enhance learner engagement, motivation, and retention. Gamification is the integration of game elements and mechanics into non-game contexts, such as educational settings, with the aim of creating an immersive and enjoyable learning experience.

Gamification taps into the inherent human desire for challenge, competition, achievement, and rewards. By incorporating game-like elements, instructional designers can transform the learning process into a more interactive and engaging journey. Learners become active participants who are motivated to overcome challenges, acquire new knowledge and skills, and achieve a sense of accomplishment.

One of the key benefits of gamification in instructional design is its ability to enhance learner engagement. Games provide a stimulating and interactive environment that captures learners' attention and maintains their focus. Through gamification, instructional designers can introduce captivating narratives, meaningful quests, and challenging tasks that immerse learners in the learning experience. By infusing elements of exploration, discovery, and problem-solving, gamification keeps learners actively involved and invested in their own learning journey.

Gamification also fosters intrinsic motivation among learners. By incorporating elements such as badges, leaderboards, points, and levels, instructional designers create a sense of achievement and progression. Learners feel a sense of accomplishment as they earn rewards, unlock new challenges, and track their progress. This intrinsic motivation encourages learners to persist, overcome obstacles, and strive for continuous improvement.

Furthermore, gamification promotes a sense of healthy competition and social interaction. Leaderboards and competitive challenges inspire learners to perform their best and compare their progress with peers. Collaborative games and team-based activities foster cooperation, communication, and peer learning. Gamification creates a supportive learning community where learners can interact, share insights, and celebrate achievements together.

The integration of gamification in instructional design also enhances the retention of knowledge and skills. Games provide opportunities for active practice, immediate feedback, and reinforcement of learning objectives. Through gamification, learners engage in repeated practice, face challenges, and receive timely feedback on their performance. This iterative process reinforces learning, helps solidify concepts, and promotes long-term retention.

However, it is important for instructional designers to approach gamification with careful consideration. Gamification should not be used merely as a superficial layer of game-like elements added to the learning experience. Instead, instructional designers should align game mechanics with the learning objectives, content, and desired outcomes. The gamified elements should be purposefully designed to support the instructional goals and enhance the learning process.

Technology plays a significant role in implementing gamification in instructional design. Learning management systems, online platforms, and educational apps provide a platform for gamified experiences. These technologies enable instructional designers to create interactive interfaces, track learner progress, and offer personalized feedback. Additionally, the use of mobile devices, augmented reality, and virtual reality can further enhance the gamified learning experience, making it more immersive and interactive.

In conclusion, gamification has the potential to revolutionize instructional design by transforming learning into an engaging and immersive experience. By integrating game elements, instructional designers can harness the power of motivation, challenge, and rewards to create dynamic learning environments. Gamification enhances learner engagement, fosters intrinsic motivation, promotes collaboration, and improves knowledge retention. When implemented thoughtfully and aligned with the instructional goals, gamification can unlock learners' potential, create memorable learning experiences, and inspire a lifelong love for learning.

Gamification Strategies for Effective Learning

In this chapter, we delve deeper into the strategies and best practices for implementing gamification in instructional design to ensure effective learning outcomes. While gamification offers exciting opportunities to engage learners and enhance their motivation, it is essential to employ thoughtful strategies to maximize its potential and create meaningful learning experiences.

Define Clear Learning Objectives: Before incorporating gamification, instructional designers must clearly define the learning objectives they want to achieve. The gamified elements should align with these objectives and support the desired learning outcomes. By establishing clear goals, instructional designers can design game mechanics that directly contribute to learners' progress and skill development.

Understand the Target Audience: Successful gamification requires an understanding of the target audience's preferences, motivations, and learning styles. Conducting learner analysis and gathering feedback can provide valuable insights into learners' interests, challenges, and expectations. Tailoring the gamified elements to align with learners' preferences increases engagement and fosters a personalized learning experience.

Integrate Storytelling and Narrative: Incorporating storytelling elements in gamification can create a compelling context for learning. A well-crafted narrative engages learners emotionally, provides context for challenges, and creates a sense of purpose. By immersing learners in an engaging storyline, instructional designers can make the learning experience more relatable, memorable, and impactful.

Provide Clear Instructions and Guidance: While gamification aims to foster autonomy and exploration, clear instructions and guidance are crucial for learners to understand the rules, mechanics, and objectives. Instructional designers should provide clear and concise instructions at the beginning of the gamified experience and offer ongoing support whenever necessary. Clear guidance ensures that learners understand the purpose and rules of the game, reducing frustration and enhancing their overall experience.

Incorporate Meaningful Challenges: Gamification should present learners with meaningful challenges that require critical thinking, problem-solving, and application of knowledge. Challenges should be designed to be progressively more difficult, allowing learners to build upon their skills and knowledge. Balancing the difficulty level is essential to keep learners engaged without overwhelming them. Additionally, incorporating real-world scenarios and authentic challenges makes the learning experience more relevant and applicable.

Provide Immediate and Constructive Feedback: Timely and constructive feedback is crucial in gamified learning experiences. Learners should receive feedback on their progress, performance, and decision-making throughout the game. Positive reinforcement, such as badges, points, or virtual rewards, can motivate learners to persist and achieve higher levels of mastery. Additionally, constructive feedback should guide learners' reflection, highlight areas for improvement, and offer suggestions for further learning.

Foster Collaboration and Competition: Gamification can leverage the power of social interaction by fostering collaboration and healthy competition. Incorporating multiplayer elements, team challenges, or leaderboards encourages learners to collaborate, share knowledge, and support each other's learning. Competition can be used as a motivational tool to encourage learners to strive for improvement, but it should be balanced to avoid creating a stressful or demotivating environment.

Track Progress and Provide Progression Paths: Gamification should provide learners with a sense of progression and achievement. Tracking learners' progress through levels, achievements, or progress bars gives them a visual representation of their growth and encourages them to continue advancing. Additionally, offering branching paths or personalized learning journeys based on learners' performance and preferences can enhance engagement and provide a customized learning experience.

Reflect and Iterate: Continuously evaluate the effectiveness of the gamification strategies and iterate based on learner feedback and performance data. Analyze learners' engagement, progress, and learning outcomes to identify areas for improvement and adjust game mechanics accordingly. Regularly updating and enhancing the gamified experience keeps it fresh, relevant, and aligned with learners' evolving needs.

engage learners and facilitate effective learning outcomes. Gamification, when implemented thoughtfully, can transform the learning experience by tapping into learners' intrinsic motivation, promoting active participation, and fostering a sense of achievement.

Balance Challenges and Rewards: It is crucial to strike a balance between challenges and rewards in a gamified learning experience. While challenges provide opportunities for growth and learning, rewards serve as incentives and reinforce positive behaviors. Instructional designers should ensure that challenges are challenging enough to maintain learner interest and motivation, while rewards are meaningful and aligned with the learning objectives. This balance encourages a sense of accomplishment and prevents learners from becoming overly focused on extrinsic rewards.

Offer Multiple Pathways and Choices: Gamification can benefit from providing learners with multiple pathways and choices to navigate through the learning experience. This approach empowers learners to take ownership of their learning journey and tailor it to their preferences. By offering different options, branching paths, or alternative activities, instructional designers promote learner autonomy, engagement, and a sense of control over their learning experience.

Foster Reflection and Application: Gamified learning experiences should include opportunities for reflection and application of knowledge. After completing challenges or levels, learners should be encouraged to reflect on what they have learned and how it can be applied in real-life situations. This reflection deepens understanding, promotes critical thinking, and facilitates the transfer of knowledge and skills to practical contexts.

Encourage Peer Interaction and Collaboration: Incorporating social elements into gamification enhances the learning experience by promoting peer interaction and collaboration. By including multiplayer features, discussion forums, or collaborative challenges, learners can engage with their peers, share insights, and learn from each other. Collaboration not only enriches the learning process but also fosters teamwork, communication, and the development of interpersonal skills.

Incorporate Real-Time Feedback: Providing real-time feedback during gamified activities enhances the learning experience by offering immediate guidance and reinforcement. Feedback can be in the form of hints, tips, or suggestions that help learners overcome challenges and improve their performance. Real-time feedback allows learners to make adjustments, correct misconceptions, and continue learning without delay, maximizing their progress and growth.

Celebrate Milestones and Achievements: Recognizing and celebrating learners' milestones and achievements is a powerful motivator in gamified learning experiences. Instructional designers can incorporate virtual badges, certificates, or special rewards to mark significant progress or mastery of specific skills. Celebrating achievements not only boosts learners' confidence and self-esteem but also reinforces their dedication to the learning journey.

By implementing these strategies, instructional designers can create gamified learning experiences that captivate learners, fuel their intrinsic motivation, and facilitate effective learning outcomes. Gamification has the potential to revolutionize instructional design by transforming the traditional learning process into an engaging and interactive adventure. Through carefully crafted game mechanics, meaningful challenges, and purposeful rewards, instructional designers can leverage gamification to empower learners, foster deep understanding, and inspire a lifelong love for learning.

The Power of Instructional Design

In the vast universe of education, instructional design stands as a beacon of hope, a catalyst for change, and a force that shapes the very fabric of learning. In this final chapter, we embark on a heartfelt exploration of the profound impact and emotional significance of instructional design. It is a chapter that invites us to reflect on our journey, to honor the transformative power of education, and to celebrate the boundless possibilities that lie ahead.

Imagine a world where education is not confined to the walls of a classroom, but permeates every aspect of our lives—a world where every learner, regardless of age or background, has access to quality education that ignites their passions and nurtures their potential. Instructional design holds the key to unlocking this vision—a vision of equity, empowerment, and lifelong learning.

As instructional designers, we are guardians of knowledge, architects of inspiration, and catalysts of change. We have the power to shape the learning experiences of individuals, communities, and even societies. Every decision we make, every design choice we implement, has the potential to ignite a spark of curiosity, to empower a learner's voice, and to create a ripple effect of positive transformation.

In this final chapter, we reflect on the emotional significance of instructional design. We celebrate the moments of connection and inspiration, where learners' eyes light up with understanding and their hearts fill with a thirst for knowledge. We honor the profound responsibility that comes with our role—the responsibility to nurture the intellectual, emotional, and social growth of our learners.

But beyond the immediate impact, we also delve into the far-reaching consequences of instructional design. We acknowledge the potential to shape future generations, to foster empathy and understanding, and to cultivate a generation of changemakers who will tackle the complex challenges of our world with compassion and ingenuity.

Moreover, we recognize that instructional design is not a static field—it evolves, adapts, and transforms in response to the changing needs and realities of our learners. We embrace the emotional journey of growth, the exhilaration of exploring new technologies and pedagogies, and the joy of discovering innovative approaches that redefine the boundaries of education.

So, let us celebrate the power of instructional design—the power to inspire, to empower, and to transform lives. Let us honor the emotional connection between educators and learners, recognizing that at the heart of every instructional design is a desire to create meaningful and impactful learning experiences.

As we conclude our journey through the ADDIE method, let us carry forward the lessons learned, the insights gained, and the passion ignited. Let us continue to explore, to innovate, and to advocate for a future where education knows no bounds—a future where the transformative power of instructional design reaches every corner of the globe, lighting the way for generations to come.

This is the power of instructional design—the power to shape minds, hearts, and the world.

45

Implementing Effective Instructional Strategies

In this chapter, we delve into the art of implementing effective instructional strategies. We explore a range of pedagogical approaches, from traditional to innovative, and examine their emotional impact on learners. We discuss the importance of creating a positive and inclusive learning environment, fostering engagement, and promoting active learning. Through the careful selection and application of instructional strategies, we can ignite a passion for learning and empower learners to achieve their full potential.

In this chapter, we delve into the art of implementing effective instructional strategies. We recognize that the selection and application of instructional strategies play a crucial role in shaping the emotional experience of learners. By thoughtfully designing and implementing strategies that cater to diverse learning needs, we can create engaging, meaningful, and impactful learning experiences.

One of the fundamental considerations when implementing instructional strategies is to ensure alignment with the learning objectives. Each strategy should be carefully chosen based on its ability to support and enhance the desired outcomes of the instructional design. This alignment cultivates a sense of purpose and relevance, igniting the emotional connection between learners and the content they are engaging with.

In addition to alignment, the emotional impact of instructional strategies is profoundly influenced by their level of interactivity and learner engagement. Strategies that actively involve learners in the learning process, such as group discussions, hands-on activities, and problem-solving exercises, have the potential to evoke a sense of ownership, empowerment, and excitement. When learners are actively engaged, their emotional investment in the learning experience deepens, resulting in increased motivation and a heightened sense of fulfillment.

Furthermore, the emotional impact of instructional strategies is closely tied to the level of challenge they present to learners. Striking the right balance between challenge and support is crucial to foster a positive emotional climate within the learning environment. When learners are appropriately challenged, they experience a sense of accomplishment and self-efficacy, which in turn fuels their intrinsic motivation and desire to continue learning.

The emotional dimension of instructional strategies also extends to the incorporation of multimedia elements and sensory stimuli. Visuals, audio, and interactive media can evoke powerful emotional responses, capturing learners' attention, stimulating their senses, and creating a lasting impact. Well-designed multimedia elements have the potential to trigger emotions such as curiosity, excitement, and empathy, enhancing the overall learning experience.

Another aspect to consider when implementing instructional strategies is the importance of providing timely and constructive feedback. Feedback serves as a valuable emotional guidepost for learners, offering guidance, affirmation, and opportunities for growth. It fosters a sense of connection between learners and their progress, instilling confidence and promoting a growth mindset. Thoughtful and personalized feedback has the potential to nurture learners' emotional well-being, encouraging them to persevere, take risks, and embrace continuous improvement.

Finally, the emotional impact of instructional strategies is deeply influenced by the learning environment itself. Creating a positive, inclusive, and supportive atmosphere is essential for learners to feel safe, valued, and comfortable to take risks and actively engage in the learning process. Instructional strategies that foster collaboration, encourage diverse perspectives, and promote a sense of belonging contribute to an emotionally rich learning environment that nurtures learners' overall well-being.

In conclusion, the implementation of effective instructional strategies is a dynamic interplay of alignment, interactivity, challenge, multimedia, feedback, and a supportive learning environment. By harnessing these elements and considering their emotional impact, we can create transformative learning experiences that inspire, empower, and connect learners on a profound level. The emotional journey of learners is intricately intertwined with the strategies we choose, and by embracing this emotional dimension, we unlock the full potential of instructional design to shape minds, hearts, and lives.

Leveraging Technology for Enhanced Learning Experiences

In this chapter, we explore the powerful intersection of instructional design and technology. We recognize the transformative potential of technology to enhance learning experiences, engage learners on a deeper emotional level, and open doors to new realms of knowledge and collaboration.

The rapid advancement of technology has revolutionized the way we access information, communicate, and interact with the world around us. Within the realm of education, technology has become an invaluable tool for instructional designers, offering innovative ways to engage learners, expand their horizons, and bridge geographical boundaries. One of the key advantages of leveraging technology in instructional design is its ability to increase accessibility and inclusivity. Technology can provide diverse learners with personalized learning experiences, accommodating their unique needs, preferences, and learning styles. Whether through assistive technologies for learners with disabilities or adaptive learning platforms that adjust content based on individual progress, technology has the potential to create emotionally inclusive environments that empower learners to overcome barriers and thrive.

Furthermore, technology offers a wealth of multimedia resources that can evoke strong emotional responses and deepen learners' engagement. The use of interactive simulations, virtual reality, videos, and gamified elements can transport learners to new contexts, spark their curiosity, and elicit emotional connections with the content. Immersive and interactive experiences facilitated by technology have the power to evoke emotions such as excitement, awe, empathy, and wonder, fostering a profound and lasting impact on the learning process.

Collaboration and communication are also greatly enhanced through technology. Online platforms, discussion boards, video conferencing, and social media enable learners to connect and collaborate with peers from diverse backgrounds and geographical locations. These digital spaces create opportunities for emotional connections, shared experiences, and the exchange of ideas and perspectives. Technology-supported collaboration fosters a sense of belonging, community, and collective growth, enriching the emotional fabric of the learning journey.

Moreover, technology can provide immediate and personalized feedback, offering learners valuable insights into their progress and achievements. Automated assessment tools, adaptive quizzes, and data analytics enable instructional designers to provide timely and constructive feedback that guides learners' growth, instills confidence, and encourages self-reflection. The emotional impact of feedback is amplified when learners receive personalized and specific guidance, reinforcing their sense of accomplishment, motivation, and continuous improvement.

As instructional designers navigate the vast landscape of educational technology, it is crucial to approach its integration with careful consideration. The selection and integration of technology should be driven by the learning objectives, pedagogical principles, and the needs of the learners. It is essential to strike a balance between leveraging technology's capabilities while preserving the human connection and emotional engagement within the learning process.

In conclusion, the integration of technology into instructional design opens up a world of possibilities, enriching the emotional dimensions of learning experiences. Through technology, we can create inclusive, interactive, and immersive environments that foster curiosity, empathy, collaboration, and personal growth. When harnessed thoughtfully, technology becomes a catalyst for emotional engagement, expanding the boundaries of learning and empowering learners to embrace the future with confidence and resilience.

Cultivating Inclusive Learning Environments

In this chapter, we delve into the importance of cultivating inclusive learning environments within the realm of instructional design. We recognize that creating an environment where every learner feels valued, respected, and supported is essential for fostering emotional well-being, promoting effective learning, and nurturing a sense of belonging.

Inclusion goes beyond mere accessibility; it encompasses a holistic approach that celebrates diversity, embraces individual differences, and creates opportunities for equitable participation. Instructional designers have a pivotal role in shaping these environments, ensuring that all learners, regardless of their background, abilities, or identities, can thrive and succeed.

One of the foundational principles of cultivating an inclusive learning environment is the recognition and affirmation of diverse perspectives and experiences. By incorporating diverse voices, cultural references, and examples into instructional materials and activities, we create an emotionally rich and responsive environment that acknowledges and values the lived experiences of all learners. This not only promotes a sense of inclusion but also enhances learners' emotional connection to the content, making it more relatable, meaningful, and engaging.

Building empathy and fostering a culture of respect and understanding are also essential components of an inclusive learning environment. Instructional designers can integrate opportunities for learners to explore different perspectives, engage in respectful dialogue, and collaborate on projects that celebrate diversity. By promoting empathy, learners develop emotional intelligence, cultural competence, and a deep appreciation for the richness that diversity brings to the learning experience.

Another critical aspect of inclusivity is designing instruction that caters to the diverse learning needs of individuals. This involves considering different learning styles, preferences, and abilities when selecting instructional strategies, materials, and assessments. By offering multiple pathways for engagement and expression, instructional designers empower learners to showcase their strengths and talents, fostering a sense of confidence, self-esteem, and competence.

Creating a safe and supportive learning environment is paramount to cultivating inclusivity. Instructional designers can establish norms and guidelines that promote respectful behavior, active listening, and collaboration. They can also foster positive teacher-learner and learner-learner relationships by encouraging open communication, providing timely feedback, and nurturing a sense of trust. When learners feel safe and supported, they are more likely to take risks, ask questions, and fully engage in the learning process.

Furthermore, instructional designers can leverage technology to enhance inclusivity within learning environments. Digital platforms can offer features that support accessibility, such as closed captioning, screen reader compatibility, and alternative formats. Online discussion forums and collaborative tools enable learners to engage in conversations and activities at their own pace, facilitating meaningful participation regardless of geographical location or time constraints. Technology can be a powerful tool for bridging barriers and ensuring that no learner is left behind.

In conclusion, cultivating inclusive learning environments is a fundamental responsibility of instructional designers. By embracing diversity, fostering empathy, designing for diverse learning needs, and creating safe and supportive spaces, instructional designers can nurture emotionally inclusive environments where all learners can thrive, learn, and grow. Inclusive learning environments empower learners to celebrate their unique identities, connect with others on a profound level, and contribute to a more inclusive and equitable society. Through their work, instructional designers have the opportunity to shape not only the minds but also the hearts of learners, fostering a sense of belonging, empathy, and compassion that extends far beyond the classroom walls.

Assessing Learning Outcomes

In this chapter, we explore the critical role of assessment in the instructional design process. Assessing learning outcomes is not only a means to evaluate learners' knowledge and skills but also a powerful tool for promoting emotional growth, building self-confidence, and fostering a sense of achievement.

Assessment serves as a guidepost, providing valuable feedback to both learners and instructional designers. By aligning assessments with the intended learning outcomes, instructional designers can gain insights into the effectiveness of their instructional strategies and make informed decisions about adjustments and improvements. At the same time, learners receive feedback on their progress, enabling them to gauge their understanding, identify areas for improvement, and celebrate their accomplishments.

One of the key considerations in assessment design is authenticity. Authentic assessments mirror real-world tasks and challenges, allowing learners to apply their knowledge and skills in meaningful contexts. By presenting learners with authentic scenarios, problems, or projects, instructional designers create emotionally engaging assessments that tap into learners' intrinsic motivation, relevance, and sense of purpose. Authentic assessments not only evaluate learners' mastery but also foster deeper understanding, critical thinking, and the development of transferable skills.

In addition to authenticity, assessment methods that offer multiple forms of expression and varied pathways to demonstrate learning are crucial for promoting inclusivity and emotional well-being. Recognizing that learners have diverse strengths, preferences, and learning styles, instructional designers can provide a range of assessment options. This could include written assignments, oral presentations, multimedia projects, performances, and collaborative group work. Offering these options allows learners to showcase their knowledge and skills in ways that resonate with their unique abilities and talents, instilling a sense of pride, self-worth, and accomplishment.

Formative assessment plays a pivotal role in supporting learners' emotional well-being and growth throughout the learning process. By providing ongoing feedback, instructional designers help learners understand their strengths, areas for improvement, and growth potential. Timely and constructive feedback cultivates a growth mindset, encouraging learners to persist, take risks, and embrace continuous learning. By focusing on the process rather than just the final outcome, formative assessment nurtures a sense of resilience, self-reflection, and the belief that with effort and perseverance, progress is possible.

The emotional impact of assessment is also influenced by the fairness and transparency of the evaluation process. Clear assessment criteria, rubrics, and grading guidelines provide learners with a sense of clarity and predictability. When learners understand how their work will be evaluated and the standards they are striving to meet, it reduces anxiety, promotes a sense of fairness, and encourages a growth-oriented mindset. Additionally, involving learners in the assessment process, such as self-assessment or peer assessment, fosters metacognitive skills, reflection, and a deeper understanding of their own learning journey.

Furthermore, instructional designers can leverage technology to enhance the assessment process. Online quizzes, automated grading tools, and data analytics offer efficient ways to collect and analyze assessment data. Technology can also provide opportunities for interactive and immersive assessments, such as simulations or virtual reality experiences. These innovative assessment methods not only capture learners' attention but also provide immediate feedback and opportunities for reflection, enriching the emotional experience of the assessment process.

In conclusion, assessment is not solely a means to measure learning outcomes but a powerful vehicle for emotional growth, self-reflection, and celebration of achievements. By designing authentic, inclusive, and formative assessments, instructional designers create opportunities for learners to demonstrate their knowledge, skills, and personal growth. When assessments are aligned with the intended outcomes, offer multiple forms of expression, provide timely and constructive feedback, and promote fairness and transparency, they become transformative experiences that empower learners to take ownership of their learning journey, embrace challenges, and realize their full potential.

Evaluating Instructional Design Effectiveness

In this chapter, we explore the importance of evaluating the effectiveness of instructional design and its impact on learner outcomes. We recognize that evaluation is a critical component of the instructional design process, providing valuable insights into the strengths and weaknesses of instructional materials, strategies, and overall design.

Evaluation serves as a means to determine the extent to which instructional goals and objectives have been achieved. By systematically assessing the effectiveness of instructional design, instructional designers can make informed decisions about instructional revisions, improvements, and future iterations. Evaluation provides a feedback loop that drives continuous improvement, ensuring that instructional materials and strategies align with learner needs, meet desired outcomes, and remain relevant in a rapidly evolving educational landscape.

One of the key aspects of evaluating instructional design effectiveness is the selection of appropriate evaluation methods and measures. Instructional designers must align evaluation methods with the intended outcomes and consider the specific context and constraints of the learning environment. Evaluation methods may include pre- and post-tests, surveys, interviews, observations, and performance assessments. By using a combination of quantitative and qualitative data, instructional designers can gain a comprehensive understanding of the impact of their instructional design choices.

Formative evaluation, conducted during the design and development process, allows instructional designers to gather feedback and make necessary adjustments before implementing the instruction. This ongoing evaluation helps identify potential issues, refine instructional strategies, and ensure that the design aligns with the intended goals. Formative evaluation involves soliciting feedback from learners, subject matter experts, and other stakeholders to validate the instructional design choices and ensure that they effectively address the learning needs.

Summative evaluation, conducted after the implementation of the instruction, focuses on assessing the overall effectiveness of the instructional design. This evaluation provides a comprehensive assessment of learner outcomes and the extent to which the instructional design has achieved its intended goals. Summative evaluation data informs decisions about the overall success of the instructional design and provides valuable insights for future improvements.

Instructional designers must also consider the emotional impact of evaluation on learners. Evaluation should be designed in a way that minimizes anxiety and stress, while maximizing opportunities for reflection, self-assessment, and celebration of achievements. Providing clear evaluation criteria, offering constructive feedback, and emphasizing the growth mindset can help learners perceive evaluation as a supportive and motivating process rather than a judgment of their abilities. By fostering a positive emotional experience during evaluation, instructional designers promote learner engagement, motivation, and a sense of self-efficacy.

Furthermore, technology can play a significant role in evaluating instructional design effectiveness. Learning management systems, analytics tools, and data visualization platforms can provide valuable insights into learner progress, engagement, and achievement. Technology enables instructional designers to collect, analyze, and interpret data more efficiently, allowing for data-driven decision-making and targeted interventions. Technology also offers opportunities for adaptive assessment, where assessments are dynamically tailored to learners' individual needs, providing personalized feedback and support.

In conclusion, evaluating instructional design effectiveness is crucial for ensuring that instructional materials and strategies meet desired outcomes and learner needs. By conducting formative and summative evaluations, instructional designers gain insights into the strengths and weaknesses of their designs, make informed decisions for improvement, and contribute to the continuous enhancement of the learning experience. By selecting appropriate evaluation methods, considering the emotional impact of evaluation, and leveraging technology, instructional designers can create a culture of evidence-based decision-making and drive positive educational outcomes. Through effective evaluation, instructional designers have the power to transform instructional design and enhance the educational experiences of learners.

Collaborative Learning and Instructional Design

In this chapter, we delve into the concept of collaborative learning and its significance in instructional design. Collaborative learning is an approach that emphasizes active participation, cooperation, and knowledge sharing among learners. It harnesses the power of social interaction to enhance learning outcomes, critical thinking, problem-solving skills, and interpersonal communication.

Understanding Collaborative Learning: Collaborative learning involves learners working together in groups or teams to achieve common learning goals. It promotes peer interaction, shared responsibility, and the exchange of ideas, perspectives, and knowledge. Through collaborative activities, learners engage in discussions, debates, and collaborative problem-solving, fostering a deeper understanding of the subject matter.

Benefits of Collaborative Learning: Collaborative learning offers numerous benefits to learners. It encourages active engagement, as learners take an active role in their own learning process rather than being passive recipients of information. Collaborative learning also enhances critical thinking skills as learners analyze, evaluate, and construct knowledge collectively. Moreover, it improves communication skills, as learners engage in discussions, negotiate ideas, and articulate their thoughts.

Designing Collaborative Learning Activities: When designing collaborative learning activities, instructional designers should consider several key factors. These include establishing clear learning objectives, defining group roles and responsibilities, creating a supportive and inclusive learning environment, and providing appropriate guidance and facilitation. It is important to strike a balance between structure and autonomy to ensure that learners collaborate effectively while still having the freedom to explore and contribute their unique perspectives.

Promoting Effective Collaboration: To promote effective collaboration, instructional designers can incorporate various strategies. These include providing clear instructions and guidelines for collaboration, fostering a positive and respectful learning culture, encouraging active participation from all group members, and facilitating opportunities for reflection and feedback. Creating a sense of shared ownership and accountability within the group can also enhance the collaborative learning experience.

Technology-Enabled Collaborative Learning: Technology plays a crucial role in facilitating collaborative learning. Online platforms, discussion forums, video conferencing tools, and collaborative document editing tools provide opportunities for learners to collaborate regardless of geographical constraints. Instructional designers can leverage these technologies to create virtual collaborative spaces where learners can interact, share resources, and collaborate on projects.

Assessing Collaborative Learning: Assessing collaborative learning requires a thoughtful approach. Traditional individual assessments may not fully capture the value of collaboration. Instead, instructional designers can use a combination of individual and group assessments. Individual assessments can evaluate learners' understanding and application of knowledge, while group assessments can focus on evaluating the effectiveness of collaboration, such as the ability to communicate, cooperate, and contribute to the group's goals.

Overcoming Challenges: Collaborative learning can present challenges, such as differences in learning styles, personality conflicts, or varying levels of contribution from group members. Instructional designers should anticipate and address these challenges by promoting clear communication, fostering a positive and inclusive learning culture, and providing strategies for conflict resolution and effective teamwork.

Real-World Applications: Collaborative learning has real-world applications beyond the classroom. In professional settings, collaborative skills are highly valued as they contribute to effective teamwork, innovation, and problem-solving. Instructional designers can design collaborative learning experiences that mirror real-world scenarios, allowing learners to develop skills that are directly applicable to their future careers.

In conclusion, collaborative learning is a powerful instructional approach that fosters active engagement, critical thinking, and interpersonal skills. By designing collaborative learning experiences, instructional designers can create dynamic and interactive learning environments that promote knowledge sharing, cooperation, and deeper understanding. Collaborative learning prepares learners for the challenges of the real world, equipping them with the skills necessary for effective collaboration and lifelong learning.

Measuring the Impact of Instructional Design

In this chapter, we explore the importance of measuring the impact of instructional design and the various approaches and methods used to assess the effectiveness of instructional interventions. Measuring the impact allows instructional designers to evaluate the success of their designs, identify areas for improvement, and make data-driven decisions to enhance the learning experience.

The Significance of Measuring Impact: Measuring the impact of instructional design is essential for several reasons. It provides valuable insights into the effectiveness of instructional strategies, materials, and activities. By gathering data and evidence, instructional designers can determine whether their interventions are achieving the desired learning outcomes and meeting the needs of the learners. Measuring impact also helps in justifying investments in instructional design and informing future design decisions.

Setting Clear Learning Objectives and Outcomes: Measuring impact starts with setting clear and measurable learning objectives and outcomes. Instructional designers should define specific goals and expected learning outcomes that align with the overall purpose of the instruction. Clear objectives provide a basis for measuring the impact by comparing learners' performance before and after the instructional intervention.

Choosing Appropriate Assessment Methods: Various assessment methods can be employed to measure the impact of instructional design. These methods may include pre- and post-tests, quizzes, observations, interviews, surveys, and performance evaluations. Instructional designers should select assessment methods that align with the learning objectives and allow for the collection of meaningful and reliable data.

Collecting Quantitative and Qualitative Data: Measuring impact involves collecting both quantitative and qualitative data. Quantitative data provides numerical insights, such as scores, completion rates, or time spent on tasks, allowing for statistical analysis and comparisons. Qualitative data, on the other hand, captures learners' perceptions, experiences, and feedback, providing valuable insights into the instructional design's effectiveness from a subjective perspective.

Analyzing Data and Drawing Conclusions: Once data is collected, instructional designers must analyze it to draw meaningful conclusions about the impact of their designs. Statistical analysis of quantitative data can reveal patterns, trends, and significant differences, while qualitative data analysis involves coding, categorizing, and interpreting learners' responses. By triangulating quantitative and qualitative data, instructional designers can gain a comprehensive understanding of the impact of their instructional interventions.

Iterating and Improving Instructional Design: Measuring impact is an iterative process that allows instructional designers to refine and improve their designs. By analyzing the data, identifying areas for improvement, and making data-driven decisions, instructional designers can iterate on their designs to enhance the learning experience. This continuous improvement cycle ensures that instructional interventions are effective, engaging, and aligned with learners' needs.

Considering Stakeholder Feedback: In addition to data analysis, gathering feedback from stakeholders, including learners, instructors, and administrators, is valuable for measuring impact. Stakeholder feedback provides insights into the usability, relevance, and effectiveness of the instructional design. Surveys, interviews, focus groups, and user testing can be employed to gather this feedback, allowing instructional designers to gain a holistic understanding of the impact.

Long-Term Impact Assessment: Measuring the impact of instructional design should not be limited to immediate outcomes. Long-term impact assessment involves evaluating the durability and transferability of the acquired knowledge and skills over time. Instructional designers can employ follow-up assessments, surveys, or interviews to determine the long-term impact of the instructional intervention and identify areas where reinforcement or additional support may be needed.

By implementing robust measurement strategies, instructional designers can gain valuable insights into the effectiveness of their designs and make informed decisions to enhance the learning experience. Measuring impact ensures that instructional interventions are aligned with the desired learning outcomes, promote learner success, and contribute to the overall effectiveness of the educational process.

Continuous Improvement in Instructional Design

In this chapter, we explore the concept of continuous improvement in instructional design and its importance in creating effective and impactful learning experiences. Continuous improvement involves an ongoing process of reflection, evaluation, and refinement to enhance instructional design strategies, materials, and activities.

The Value of Continuous Improvement: Continuous improvement is crucial in instructional design as it allows for the identification of areas for enhancement and the implementation of iterative changes. By continuously evaluating and refining instructional interventions, instructional designers can ensure that the learning experience remains relevant, engaging, and aligned with the evolving needs of the learners.

Embracing a Reflective Practice: Reflective practice is a fundamental component of continuous improvement in instructional design. Instructional designers should engage in self-reflection, critically examining their designs, implementation strategies, and outcomes. Reflection allows for the identification of strengths and weaknesses, enabling instructional designers to make informed decisions for improvement.

Gathering and Analyzing Feedback: Feedback from learners, instructors, and other stakeholders is invaluable in the continuous improvement process. Instructional designers should actively seek feedback through surveys, interviews, focus groups, or user testing. This feedback provides insights into learners' experiences, preferences, and challenges, helping identify areas for refinement and enhancement.

Data-Driven Decision Making: Continuous improvement in instructional design relies on data-driven decision making. Instructional designers should collect and analyze relevant data to inform their decisions. This data may include assessment results, learning analytics, user feedback, or performance metrics. By examining data trends and patterns, instructional designers can identify areas of improvement and implement evidence-based changes.

Collaboration and Professional Development: Collaboration among instructional designers, instructors, and other stakeholders is essential for continuous improvement. By fostering a collaborative environment, instructional designers can share insights, exchange ideas, and learn from one another. Additionally, engaging in professional development activities, attending conferences, and participating in communities of practice contribute to professional growth and the acquisition of new knowledge and skills.

Iterative Design Processes: Continuous improvement involves iterative design processes that allow instructional designers to refine and enhance their interventions.

Instructional designers can use models such as the ADDIE (Analysis, Design, Development, Implementation, Evaluation) or SAM (Successive Approximation Model) to guide the iterative design process. These models emphasize ongoing evaluation and revision at each stage of the instructional design cycle.

Incorporating Emerging Technologies: Continuous improvement also involves keeping up with emerging technologies and their potential impact on instructional design. Instructional designers should stay informed about advancements in educational technology, learning management systems, interactive tools, and multimedia resources. Integrating relevant technologies into instructional design can enhance engagement, interactivity, and learner-centeredness.

Seeking Innovation and Creativity: Continuous improvement encourages instructional designers to seek innovation and creativity in their designs. By exploring new instructional strategies, formats, or approaches, instructional designers can push the boundaries of traditional design practices. Embracing innovative and creative ideas can lead to exciting breakthroughs and more effective learning experiences.

Celebrating Successes: Recognizing and celebrating successes is an important aspect of continuous improvement. Instructional designers should acknowledge and celebrate the positive impacts of their improvements, whether it be increased learner engagement, improved learning outcomes, or positive feedback from stakeholders. Celebrating successes fosters motivation, boosts morale, and reinforces the value of continuous improvement efforts.

By embracing continuous improvement in instructional design, instructional designers can create dynamic, relevant, and effective learning experiences. Through reflective practice, gathering feedback, data-driven decision making, collaboration, and embracing innovation, instructional designers can refine their designs and make impactful changes that positively influence learners' experiences and outcomes. Continuous improvement ensures that instructional design remains a dynamic and evolving field, constantly striving to meet the needs of learners in a rapidly changing educational landscape.

Final Thoughts

As we reach the final page of this book on instructional design, we reflect on the transformative journey we have undertaken together. Throughout these chapters, we have explored various aspects of instructional design, from the foundational principles to the practical strategies that empower educators to create impactful learning experiences. We have delved into the ADDIE method, examined the incorporation of multimedia, discussed gamification and collaborative learning, and explored the measurement of impact and continuous improvement.

Instructional design is a dynamic field that continually evolves in response to advancements in technology, changes in educational paradigms, and the diverse needs of learners. As instructional designers, we have the incredible opportunity to shape the future of education by designing experiences that engage, inspire, and empower learners to reach their full potential.

The journey of instructional design is not without its challenges. It requires a deep understanding of learning theories, the ability to adapt to new technologies, and the skill to navigate the ever-changing educational landscape. However, it is through these challenges that we grow and refine our craft. We become agents of change, catalysts for innovation, and advocates for learner-centered education.

But beyond the technical aspects, instructional design is

ultimately a human endeavor. It is about connecting with learners on a profound level, understanding their unique needs, and designing experiences that ignite their passion for learning. It is about fostering a supportive and inclusive learning environment that nurtures curiosity, critical thinking, and creativity. It is about recognizing the power of education to transform lives and make a positive impact on individuals, communities, and society as a whole.

As you close this book, I invite you to carry the knowledge and insights you have gained into your own instructional design journey. Embrace the art and science of designing meaningful learning experiences. Embrace the responsibility to create inclusive, engaging, and transformative educational opportunities for all learners. And above all, embrace the boundless potential that instructional design holds to shape the future of education. May your path as an instructional designer be filled with curiosity, innovation, and a deep sense of purpose. May you continue to seek new knowledge, refine your skills, and embrace the opportunities that lie ahead. And may your dedication to the art of instructional design inspire learners to embark on their own lifelong journey of discovery, growth, and empowerment.

Thank you for joining us on this enlightening exploration of instructional design. The future of education is in your hands, and the possibilities are limitless. If you are interested in my ellaborate course on the ADDIE method, please feel free to visit my website : https://trainercentric.com

Facilitating Collaborative Learning

In this chapter, we delve into the power of collaborative learning and its impact on the instructional design process. We recognize that fostering collaboration among learners can lead to deeper understanding, higher engagement, and enhanced emotional connections to the learning experience.

Collaborative learning promotes active participation, shared responsibility, and the exchange of ideas and perspectives among learners. When learners collaborate, they have the opportunity to construct knowledge together, engage in meaningful discussions, and benefit from diverse viewpoints. Instructional designers play a vital role in creating environments and designing activities that facilitate and maximize the potential of collaborative learning.

One of the key benefits of collaborative learning is the emotional support and sense of belonging it provides. Working together in groups or teams fosters a sense of community, cooperation, and shared purpose. Learners feel supported by their peers, can seek help when needed, and experience a sense of collective achievement. This emotional connection and support contribute to a positive and inclusive learning environment, promoting motivation, engagement, and a sense of shared responsibility for success.

Collaborative learning also cultivates important social and emotional skills. Through interactions with their peers, learners develop communication skills, active listening, empathy, and the ability to work effectively in a team. These skills are essential in both academic and professional settings, and collaborative learning provides a platform for learners to practice and refine them. The emotional intelligence and interpersonal skills gained through collaborative learning are invaluable for building strong relationships, resolving conflicts, and navigating diverse social contexts.

Instructional designers can employ various strategies to facilitate collaborative learning experiences. Group projects, discussions, case studies, and problem-solving activities are just a few examples of instructional approaches that encourage collaboration. By structuring activities that require learners to work together, instructional designers create opportunities for learners to engage in meaningful interactions, negotiate meaning, and co-construct knowledge. Collaboration can take place in physical classrooms, online environments, or a combination of both, allowing for flexibility and accommodating diverse learning contexts.

Technology plays a significant role in facilitating collaborative learning, particularly in virtual or blended learning environments. Online collaboration tools, discussion forums, and collaborative documents enable learners to connect and engage with their peers regardless of geographical barriers. These digital platforms offer opportunities for asynchronous collaboration, allowing learners to contribute at their own pace and provide thoughtful input. The use of technology in collaborative learning not only enhances accessibility but also expands the possibilities for global connections and cross-cultural exchanges, fostering a rich and diverse collaborative experience.

It is important to note that effective facilitation is crucial for successful collaborative learning. Instructional designers can provide clear guidelines, establish norms for respectful and inclusive participation, and offer support and guidance throughout the collaborative process. They can also encourage reflection and self-assessment, allowing learners to evaluate their own contributions and provide feedback to their peers. By modeling effective collaboration and nurturing a positive and supportive learning culture, instructional designers create an environment where learners feel empowered, valued, and motivated to actively participate in collaborative learning experiences.

In conclusion, collaborative learning is a powerful instructional approach that fosters emotional connections, supports social and emotional growth, and enhances the learning experience. By promoting collaboration, instructional designers create environments that cultivate a sense of community, develop essential social and emotional skills, and provide opportunities for learners to engage in deep learning. Through collaborative learning, learners develop not only subject knowledge but also a sense of empathy, teamwork, and appreciation for diverse perspectives. As instructional designers embrace the potential of collaborative learning, they pave the way for transformative educational experiences that prepare learners for success in an interconnected and collaborative world.

www.ingramcontent.com/pod-product-compliance
Lightning Source LLC
La Vergne TN
LVHW040031190726
843490LV00014B/2748